Zayde Reeven 1,2,3

Zayde Reeven 1,2,3
And Collected Poetry

REEVE ROBERT BRENNER
With a Foreword by Neeva Kleiman

Shengold
Rockville, Maryland

ISBN 978-0-88400-354-0
Library of Congress Control Number: 2020944557

Shengold Publishers
PO Box 4193
Rockville, MD 20849 USA
800-953-9929

Printed in the United States of America

In loving memory of Jack Furmansky,
the only tzadik lamed vavnik I ever knew

Contents

Frivolity

Foreword

After a lifetime of poetry, this collection provides a mere fraction of Reeve Robert Brenner's literary output, however removed from his far better known works of scholarship and philosophy.

Meditative, he offers various variations on a theme and several changes in personas, and sees himself primarily as a hermetic poet suitably drawn to his craft for small audiences.

Some of these poems may deserve no more than a glance but others "go straight to the elastic, infinite core of time," although there may not even be a core to time or anything resembling such a thing. Elastic, however, is a feature prominent in these pages. And allusions of the infinitive appear often enough. If the reader is prepared to "get it." A number of these poems will make the reader smile. Certain ideas and certain wordplay do just that.

Perhaps no poem can be completely appreciated or even best apprehended until its music is heard, which makes the case for reading a number of these poems aloud. And for the sheer pleasure of it, listen for the sound of the antiphonal half- comic tone responsive reading litany in the poetry section entitled, "Frivolity." For its irony, it is best read aloud alternately by at minimum, two readers.

Rabbi Brenner captures a quality of the Ashkenazic ethnic historical heritage by verse sprinkled with diverse echoes that treat that heritage and historical accounts with reverence. His sensibilities, transitioning from the perception of Israel as wandering and buffeted within the pre-state Holocaust context, and then, in his youth, in his lifetime against all odds, to a homeland at last, impelled him to experiencing and recording the emotions of that period as one who lived quite consciously the in-between transition interval. Instantiated at a time—the before and after time—that is, before there was refuge and suddenly, an improbable miracle realized at last, Israel, captured in the few lines at the end of the poem "Welcoming Arms Well Armed."

We recognize the qualities, some are mutually exclusive, which make these poems uniquely Jewish, but also very much American. Words and phrases from Yiddishkeit, or from a broader range of immigrant experience; illusions and quotations from the liturgy and from the Tanakh; traditions of the Catskills, or Hollywood, are all represented here.

Neither homespun nor unadorned, his poetry presents more like snippets or tidbits cut from their contexts of a lifetime of Jewish living and Jewish thought.

These poems are not so much selected as surviving; likely more than three times the poems of this collection have been lost to revolving door moves from the years in Israel to and fro congregations and communities in the states, a number published and some unpublished but not recovered; many of family simply vanished and made evanescent by circumstance.

Harold Bloom asserts in his *The Sorrows of Jewish American Poetry*, that there could never be a major Jewish poet in English ... And nothing is more self-deceptive for any Jewish writer than the notion that he (or she) can define the Jew." But Reeve Brenner's miniseries of poetry starting with "Permeable and Singular: Defining Israel with a Sketch in Time" through to "Fragments Beyond the Shackles of Language" comes pretty close to doing just that. His poetry takes exception to the dictionaries' and encyclopedias' characterizations and definitions of the Jewish people by re-imagining and re-forming his own offerings, annotations and glosses apprehended in rhythm and imagery. And after all, rhythm and imagery are the constituents of poetry.

Brenner's poetry relies a great deal on humor often purposefully and prankishly overdoing a metaphor for the sake of a smile. His poetry written for his grand-children, the same. He likes to play with their Hebrew names by exploring their meaning and their sense of capturing each grandchild's personal reality or person-ality. They are personal poems but peoplehood poems as well. The poems are accessible and deeply reflective of a Jewish life.

You won't find much in Reeves' poetry hewing closely to conversational, casual, or a talking quality of the kind which could be arranged differently on the page making them more like memoirs. Some are conceived on pre-set paradigmatic themes, run-ning from and running toward. Some are soft, others raging. Many are reflective of an awareness of multiple traditions and multiple theories about vision, mission and revelation. They are uncommonly learned, ardent, often strikingly fervent and ecstatic; a number of entries in this collection are seemingly possessed, animated, a kind of fevered history lessons and chronicled annals rendered in poetry.

Neeva Kleiman

Folk

Zayde Reeven, One, Two, Three

ONE

My zayde Reeven lived once
not long enough to see my mother
just long enough to see
the wide white of Russia's winter once.
and a final Pesach:
racing Elijah out the door
and winning by an earlock.
wine cups diminished: one
nineteen years plus nil
not one night too soon for mom
he never knew
and me, one grandson
and one campaign for the czar.
Round one the czar won.

TWO

Exchanging country one
for chupa two
not a love thing, mind you
for Reeven's bride
but he'll have to do
granpa two
with fat flaking
garment center cigar
offcenter and hurtling
the gauntlet of his golden teeth
the same stuff which paved his streets
seven years devouring corpulent cows,
swelling on the corporal's crusade,
incanting his capitalist cabbala

granpa
while huffing sheen
on Roosevelt dimes
to pilfer little Reeven's troth
Reeven number two.
And round two to grandpa.

THREE

A third continent
a third generation
with Reeven's words
stretched out like a tether between them:
"sure", he'd say "sure,
we Jews will have a homeland
sure, and the Czar will be overthrown
and men will walk the moon."
sure thrice he'd laugh
three positives which meant a negative for him,
a dream a miracle
in which he couldn't believe
I toss the miracle back at him
like a lasso
and laughing thrice myself,
pull tight and yank my dybbik
toward me
"behold the dreamer cometh."
But Zayde, your grandson
Reeven's third child was born there
in Yerushalayim, a sabra, Zayde.
It's all come true, Zayde.
Round three to Reeven.

To Make Sacred

You ask what desecration means.

That lampshade at Yad Vashem
of tawny amber parchment
torn from a torah scroll
whose skin testifies to sizzling flesh,
once illuminated the thighs
of an ubermensch und frau,
once cast, flickering,
the holy tongue upon their
compounding frames,
their frankfurt, furth and fulda
flaying limbs,
once flung filigreed letters
of redemptive writ,
obedient Hebrew script,
to march and retreat across
shifting sweaty nazi spines
as on keeled carapaces,
rippling wavy corrugated words
in shadows
enlarging with their heavings,
fleeting with each thrust,
once projected silhouetted shapes:
thou shalt
thou shalt not.
and we,
still shaken by that shade,
might make love
in the holy city
in the holy tongue

my quill stenciling torah tropes
upon your holy of holies
a wholly holy act,
and therewith
discomfit Jerusalem's profaners
and soften the sacrilege.

Welcoming Arms Well Armed

Distal but never distant nor detached
from the initial Egypt to Canaan
archetypical departure and arrival
that first providence providing primal
proximal communal buckle and ringbolt
cohering community and continuity
fixed in our psyches like curling cables
incumbent and superposed upon them,
these more recent remnants of firestorms appeared
not from a wilderness wasteland of 40 years
as the earlier amphibious band of escapees
pre-figuring file and rank
forging forward facsimiles
into a splitting of seas
wielding bronze bayonets
for slicing a chunk of real estate
to call home and history.

Rather, these rescued remnants
blinking from the sting of consuming darkness
from an unfathomable schvartznoir blackness
into the blazing hues of white and blue
like a trance co-mingled with consciousness
like wicked dreams pouring into wakefulness
with a sudden start
thrust upon the land of refuge with an iconic
ironic blend of exhilaration and numb stolidity
digging up the graves of long-lost selves
as if probing manifold incarnations
while summoning a dé jew view channeling
the first fugitives

figured in the foremost configuration
now arriving artza and down the gangplank
to haven, hope and the keen
clasping rejoicing embracing arms
of veteran tribesmen.
And handed a rifle.

Jerusalem Word Play

Itself a put-on drollery
concealed within a metaphoric vagary
Jerusalem, a pun on behold: peace
a play-on-words yeru city
a yerusha received shalem
wholly city

Yeru – they will yet see peace
Yeru – a future peace
Shalayim – in multiplication
see now a piece of peace
two halves one peace
hello good-bye twice shalom
never knowing whether you're coming
or going, Yerushalayim

a city that plays with shalom
praises shalom
prays for shalom
whole and holy word
whole and holy city
Jerusalem
harm not her harmonies
-make whole her peace

Street Scene Jerusalem

Black Dome of the Rock Frisbees
pilpulling on their heads
a plaited corkscrew
to yank out the dybbuk
coiled around each ear
the rebbe and his eight offspring
spring off Ben Yehudah street against the light
leaping taxis respect their religious gait
while a mustached paratrooper
machine guns sunflower seeds
between the gauntlet of his marching teeth
at the coat of no color
green market Hasid
on the street.
It's Friday in Yerushalayim
prepare for Shabbat.

Nomenclature Moses

Moses
Your nomenclature lacks patrimony
Moses
Son of an innominate deity
Apocalyptic apocopated, truncated God
You sacrifice half your name to the people
And to Adonai
Pseudonym, assume a name
Denominate
the people must be brought to their
mountain
and you to yours
where you remain.
The people must have
their awesome utterance,
divine letters,
their visionary images
and you must hear
the Voice speaking
from the thornbush
calling out your summons
from the blaze of ur-lightenment.
The people must fathom
the cryptic signals
and solve the mystery
of sacred writ.
Ra-moses, Thut-moses, Ka-moses, Ah-moses
hearken to *your* El, -Moses
The people must have you Mosheh
The severe stark fervor of your mesmerizing eyes
and your laying on
of the tender warmth of your hands.

Permeable and Singular:
Defining Israel
With a Sketch in Time

A singularly distinctive hapax legomenon, Israel
A petite three syllable word, a word among words,
anomalously misconceived, muddled and
misconstrued
blurred by the dictionaries dislocated disconnected
tautologies,
in need of a corrective formulating formula
sketching her time line
so as not to further mislead by pit-a-patted
nomenclature,
by merry-go-round onomastics,
by recurvated etymologies
and tawdry redundancies
(Let us therefore encounter the pathways of time
gone by):

Sui generis therefore permeable, protean, syncretistic,
Only and solely the one of the many,
the lone example
In sync with the idiosyncratic
But seeking no haven in illusion
It has been said:
"a most peculiar people with ways of her own."
Scribes of the repeatedly replicated words and lections.
revealing and revering ancient revelations
laced with ecstatic dreams
and visions drenched with despair,
with wistfulness and resolve

making their long way
along corridors lined with haunting,
compellingly cohering codices.

Never disowning, relentlessly restoring
the shards of their heritage
likened to the remnants of their abecedaries
inscribed on crumbled potsherds
and on tattooed numbers

A people cum repository of history's civilization
Remarkably attuned to the sounds of language,
the radiance of words
And the leitmotiv occupying the recesses of the
mind's imagination
A kind of architecture yielding prosy scrolls,
memoirist mandates, indoctrinations and exhortations.

Essentially existentially and uncommon
a people prospering generations of distinctive
self definers
endlessly revisiting and re-envisioning
their own self-sanctioned
entanglements and ambiguities,
nuanced and bold and self-contradictory
realizing a rare kind of perspective
established upon an intimate divinity
and formidable intensity,
a tribe un-bowed, self affirmed, undaunted
bearing the weight of a timeless heritage
peering over generational shoulders,
beyond the display of the fields of time and place

and like tall grass servile to winds and breezes
submissive to primary strictures and scriptures
searching for transparent paths to the transcendent,
for sapientia, sophia, wisdom,
for chochma, de'ah, bina v'heskale
without confidence
never with confidence, a career invariably careening.
while unvaryingly bracing for shoahs
where every foothold everywhere gained without
conviction
and hardly a toe-hold for ages or a handle to hold on to.
Irregularly aberrant, a stray, misplaced outlier
over the centuries.

Favored for a differentia of fractured borders
splintered boundaries of solitary, solidarity and
singularity
prismatic of disconformity and abnormity
affirming undismayed its foundational truths
and the myths of sovereign words
brought forth by minds of anomalous architecture
obliquely transvesting insubordinate teachings
as much concealing as revealing
by gestures long forgotten
by memes many times refined and re- defined
like stitches reinforcing a newly mended sail
preparing her patched make-over canvass for the
journey
unyielding to the profanations by night
nor to the despairs defining the day
bearing the weight of uncertainty
sustaining fractured vectors of refuge denied

and then defiantly departing for the next unsafe harbor

-any port in a storm-
aboard any resolute ark that might weather the flood
under skies appearing in perpetuity
heavy and leaden
to snatch the passing redemptive winds
for their imperishable and unremitting
unfinished unforeseeable unfolding,
eternalized with time itself.
And for their deathless forever-dying
forever enduring voyage.
Take that! Dictionary editors.

Foreshadowing and Channeling

Another Go Of It: an endnote on Israel.
Over the centuries a people
foreshadowing and channeling imperishable images
fueling their innermost connectives and invocations
foreshadowing generations beholden to the reach of
the past
forming a whole if not a unity of coherence

Uber precosity with afflatus as no more than
expectancy,
as a given , a presumption
presenting a plethora of penetrating peculiarity,
rummaging their collective minds for the mysteries
ever assembling a sensitive semblance of strands and
strokes
establishing the guides, guards and specialized
keepers,
channeling shoftim, shomrim, rabbanim, manhigim,
dreaming in percipient counterfactuals
telling humankind more than they wanted to hear
providing spectral gritty allure to those that join us
in slivers and flashes of promise and fatefulness
and a talent for not giving up.

Foreshadowing and channeling
like rain clouds carrying the storm
with no sun in their place, no place in the sun
Careening from calamities to carnage to cremation
Eternal straw man and punching bag
as much panoptic as pan phobic
thick-skinned but sentient

layered, tangled, rhythmically complex and composite
yet perceived as periling, sinister
as a menacing singleton
to be devoured again and again by teeth fixed
like a snare in fiendish rows
ever the ready to chew on the Jew.

Foreshadowing and channeling
Reincarnated reinstantiated reinstated
through generations, through genealogies
seen as providing
more than a few ectypes to replicate
inspired utterances
word-casting in psalms and elegies
carried along by a tribe of wayfarers and way fearers
leaving behind lasting instructive Torot
on resisting dehumanization
shedding shriveling shrifts and shrouds.
And like Ezekiel bones foreshadowed and channeled
returning repeatedly to sinuous
sinewy eternal life.

Wanderings and Voyages

Ivri from ever over there
setting forth from Seir
Marching from the land of Edom
Knowing nothing of palanquin, litter or sedan
From early on tracing a vector
riding on tawny donkeys
Sitting on caparisoned camels

And soon enough embarking in NASA capsules
Dancing, floating, to the rhythms of Einstein's warps
and curves in space and time
(mere practice for voyages unto other spheres.)
Over there and everywhere
In sync with her idiosyncrasies

Seeking no haven in illusions
embracing hyper-natural verities and ancestral
meta- truths
empathic for the stranger having become one
having been one
Tentatively inhabiting the contours of mysterious
places
interspersed among visions propagating
and penetrating the recesses of her perceptions
Ivriyim ever divining signification
from their wanderings
while bending to the wind
as into the shapelessness of the void.
Ever alone on turf shaped, tromped and stomped
Upon, a tribe of poets and scribes
opening portals into shape-shifting multiple forms

like a palimpsest grafted over layers of reverberations
imposed upon decades of times and minds
in the main concealed beneath each new iteration
stored like critically encrypted messages,
like intelligencers and operatives in stealth
cramming hard won prescriptions and presentiments
onto microdots and info bits
encoded in crucial pinheads and periods
at the close of endless paragraphs
without a sof pasuk
As befitting a tribe on an eternal trip
forever attentive to the voyage of the last mad wild
zealous syllables of recorded time.
They will be there to record it.

On the Continual Chain
Coherent Cliche

A most peculiar people
say all the Hamans, as do we to us
uncharacteristic and exceptional,
abnormous and anomalous
Like a generational chain of genealogies
Composed of cyclical calibrations
of continuous eccentricity
Conceptualized by celestialized retro-calculations
Reanimating past concoctions and crystallizations
far seeing the ever recurring quirks of the inconceivable
conducing intercalated contempt and confrontations
conducing uncertainty for conceiving
aberrant nonconformities
and forever, falteringly, felled by fatigue
facing the capricious
affirming a foothold without a place
or a persuasion.

Encountering chance mechanisms
habitually countering the do-good-for-you dogmatics
disputing contrary push-back
inferences and indications
craving to be correct in precisely portrayed worlds
anomalous in the debacles claiming the airspace
Popper's false ability falsifiability criterion
or Kuhn's paradigm shift
Pink eek to the irreverent
pushing back against the threatening concepts
of status and stasis
punctuated disequilibriated equilibrium

like a particularity in persistent distress
paradigms lost and paradise never regained

Israel as the prototypical challenge
thriving on paradoxes
and the improbabilities coiled about a self-conscious
self-contrived self-consensus self-defense
channeled through the sluice gates
co-opting deviations
and salvaging discontent
from principles resisting the downward drafts
and the hapax legomenon lone examples
compounded, mixed, mingled and tightly conjoined
clapped together, lumped together,
hanging together like interlocking cables
like an enchased endowment
with conflicting and conflating
idiosyncrasies and adhocracies
specific and special and most peculiar
like an oopo out of place object in a dig.
Does not belong!
Aleph Dalid Gordon might not be smiling
Ahad Haam not at all sad
Diametrically fulfilled and not.
A most peculiar people.

Deified and Vilified

Subjected to multi-hyphenated restlessness
And to the world's focused gaze upon her
instilling characteristic clauses
of their own mesmerizing mythos and logos
self caricatured within a mist of radiant mystification
in scope, kaleidoscopic, escaping the quotidian
transcending counter the plurality
for the sake of the singularity
instantiating the panoply of profound proliferations
with no intent to cohere with the peristaltic
given without prate, given with not
a little babble and Bavel
while pushed along against their will
against other's grain
caught we know, we're told, by the rush of things.

Disfavored, dis-enamored by both sides of the equation
Left with dreams never more than brittle shards
crumbling sacred fragments
of unyielding intractable
and uncompromising proscriptions
realized as refractory wayward tropes and memes
as remains on a handful of potsherds.

Flame shaped images,
played out omnipresent and unextinguished
like the ner tamid
on aronei kodesh
obscured cryptic recondite embedded artifacts
and for knowing something
of the transparent and hint of transcendent

like a shadow of clouds gathering across the field
moving as one
with the consciousness of all being
cast above and over
as in ivri from over there
elsewhere and foreign, tramontane and exotic
over-mining and undermining
all pretense at cognizance,
every received doctrine and attainment
sagging under the weight
of their own extended metaphor
winding this way and that
like the shapelessness of the wind
even to subtle contours at the edges
and the crisscrossing curving
cunning wily parallels along the way
bequeathing a genetic coda in folios numbing
and numbering few dunderheads or Philistines
Reflecting a mosaic of upper anatomical features
echoing and channeling their fairytale forebears
invariably – until now -crouching
and encroaching on someone else's doorsteps
under unfriendly skies
extended barely the thinnest thread
of civility and tolerance
often enough keeping the entire enterprise aloft
and without an epigraph insight in sight
despite that special sense of the uncanny
at the apex of its pyramid capacity
decidedly greater than the sum of its

soul-strengthening parts
tentatively inhabiting the spaces
interspersed among visions
on turf already well tromped by ancient minds
and stomped and stamped by holy poets
and singers of song
A Zimmerman a Simon a Cohen
empathically about the stranger, the uncommon
the remarkable
emitting plaintive melodies and sorrowful sounds
having become one having been one
in evocations of inspiration, retrospective and
introspective
remaining always and never at ease in the currents,
the idioms and the visions of the *chol*
ever true to the haunting resuscitations
and the insistent
reverberations of the *kadosh*.

Fragments Beyond
The Shackles of Language

Manifesting memorably as
Midrashic mythic messengers
Composing memories made up
of memoirs in the myriads
micro-molecules sorted on endless chains of pin-point
periods
like espionage in micro-dots, specks and dabs
Like genetic codes written within our DNA
Like artists infused with the blessings of
multiple musing muses
Releasing thought in fragments
beyond the shackles of language
While never invalidating the tribal architecture
coiled within every one of our cells
As though internally returning
to the eternity of return.

A people ever teetering imbalanced
like plate tectonics shifting underfoot
Yet never relinquishing the sovereignty of their vision
Ever opening their eyes to an inner sight-line
seeing beyond the display of the fields of time
like Einstein's warps and curves in space
so limning this people's journey through time
under the weight and in the wake
of their own penetrating metaphors.
imbued with the language of syncopations and acrostics
Often proclaimed anathema for their discourse
while riding carousels on a whirlwind of
undiminished persistence

the price and punishment
for scaling the pinnacles of transcendence.

At the Hatfield Clinical Center Chapel: Sharing Spiritual Space

I think about the holy thoughts
    Liturgies luminous with praise
I think about the prayers
    And the numinous vibes
Infusing the kadosh-pure of this hallowed locus
The energies and blessed visions
The souls which have opened up on this Sinai
And the reverence within our inward spans and spread
    A special spiritual place
The place of consecrated Oneness
I feel the aura and the benedictions calling us here
I feel human souls reflecting God's image
Embracing and exalting us here
Amid dreams and incantations of wholeness and
holiness
A softening and soothing and soul-filled station
The shared stage of sacred siblings
And so: sanctified space and home.

The Hebrew Teacher

"Not all the books
On every shelf
But what the teacher
Is herself"

Emerged at last
The buba that is in you
And with her, your own grandchildren too
To look after cleaving
Like the hem of your dress
To the canescence of your calves

In tandem, marching
As two thighs rising alternately
Beneath the guise
Draped like a self-conscious canopy
About you
Demurely place your tiny hand in mine
And off to the classroom
Swathed in your cowl,
A wholly contrived integument

Instructress and granny and child
The hickory stick
Or aufn pripichik?
At recess, at play, children swirling
Secretly in love with teacher.

Don't be too stern, schoolmistress
Don't break the little boys' hearts.
Ancient Wisdom updated:
Revere your teacher as much as heaven

Teacher, you awaken joy in their souls
Do you know that they love you?

We Are All in Love

(A wedding poem after Micah Joseph Berdichevski)
We are all in love. Everyone human.
All creatures. All things. That is part of our
creaturehood. That is
fundamental to creation. Creation is grounded in love.

It is not you alone who love, or we
or those others; all things love; and all things pour
forth
their souls.

The heavens love, the earth loves, every creature and
every living thing.
In all life, there is longing. Just as between all things
there is attraction.
Creation is itself but a longing, a kind of prayer of love.

What are clouds, the rising and setting of the sun, the
soft radiance of the moon
and the gentleness of the night? What are the flashes of
the human mind and
storms of the human heart?

These are all the songs of love of God's creation.

Zipporah: Phases and Incipient Stages.
A Midrash.

Fowl play

She swoops across his reveries
then hangs weightless in his skies
there roosts.
Once perched, expands her chest
and struts her dance
around in circles prancing,
her prismatic plumage sways
entrapping, enchanting, entrancing
forever flighty, forever fleeting
migrating koan-like tales
within her pas de un pantomime.

She emerges from her coop
to court her mate, god's coup,
sounding faint pre-echoes of resplendent
arias to come. Staples of her repertoire,
rapt, ecstatic, consecrated
interpretive interventions
attuned in timbre and tone
to the vibrating resonant
playbacks of a thornbill's mimetic calls
parlaying her ploy with song and chant
her twittering feathered cowl well wrapped about her
like talismanic talit and tfillin of a later day,
arrayed proudly, radiantly, as a crest
the most precious of ornaments.

Hovering covert within his senses she laughs
she marvels, warbles, tzip tzip orra she trills

her coy lilt cavorts line upon line
verse following verse
reconceiving choreography
for tug and beat channeling Eve
flinching rhythm, accent, and flirt simulating Sisters
one step two step box step
buck and wing, spree and fling
in triple-time pace, sashay, allemande, courante
shuffling to the ghost dance,
sun dance, snake dance, enticing ensembles
elaborate arabesque charades of her fertility dance,
to quicken and evoke his muse,
ever the most alluring avian
to bow a pinion over him.

For him, balletomane to her grand jete'
sublime, she coaxed their canon
passionately well past any lurking apostasy
furtively generative suffused with liturgical spells
pulsed with epistolary, tracts and codices
memes, tropes and interpolations
she plucked away at his soul.

Scribbling scribe, convincing script
decrypted deciphered decoded
seeding verbal foliage
with swing and stroke, chapter and verse
esoteric, exoteric offshoots
entangling sagacious sprigs
twig entwining learned flourishing twig,
parasha sidra chumash and commentary

pshat, remez, drash and sod
with withering clashing fiats
thou shalt and thou shalt not
like a feathered creature building her breach
an aerie haunt for their clannish priestly line
(and for their doomed dna)
her nest like a sanctuary an arboreal harbor
meant to be their manse and mantle
vanishing in the flickering dappled light
filtering through the brambles.

Immersed in the flow of an revenant distraction
within a mutable stead of another realm
summoning descendents
settling for transcendence
hardly enthralled by a surfeit of riffs
on cherished venerables
anticipating the measure
of a euphuistically empty reliquary
finding scant comfort in writ's consolations
not in chants nor hallowed chapels
flittering in rites, rights and sovereign sacred times
treading in metaphor, metonym, chiasm
trading in Masoretes, mappiqs and mater lectionis
trickling in descent like trees distilling light
secreting in codes and creeds
defying the tohu void
evinced in vohu emptiness.
All things, all these, overlaid, overplayed and well hidden
by the charms and pageantry of a pazair
zarkah and a tlishah gdolah.

Now, disengaging their rigadoon
past their uncannily sustaining moments
their passagework ever more spacious
her flashy screech of talons
swooshing past his ears
in breathless wondrous tempos
she unfurls slender plicated gossamer pinions
raising her coiled tendrils
uplifting as on a floating whirligig circuit
an ascension into the maw of airspace
laying claim to her own place
for her own interbeing narrative
of fair and fowl climbing
as in a deft pantomime
toward skies
where there are no remnant words
where language itself drifts away.

Clad in quickening quills
in widening hoops flutters
an apparition, phantomesque, rhapsodic
upward she glides shaping a hazy halo
forming a soft luminous loop
in concentric circles hovers
and in rings enlarging like a spiral in the glowering sky
momentarily hesitant, wavering in acclivity
as on a slight swaying tightrope
then purposefully accelerating her writhing gyre
in expanding orbits floats away.

Moshe
at the last, downcast, crestfallen, wistful
musing morose in all manner of ways
forlorn, a prophet forsaken,
his tale told by her tail
trailing an ephemeral shadow over him
abandoned now with only echoed coos
with everything to lose
with tufts and plume and nothing more
than a downy feather
to record the torah.

Fischer and Spassky

Their Esperanto chess
Not likely Yiddish
Reuven and Baruch
Bobbi and Boris
Untraditional, uncommunicative, combatants
the Dutch defense
the Straunton Gambit
forehead to forehead
is it the Little Italian Game?
Gladiators suspiciously without armor.
Not like other times and places
more than once
hunched over frigid
more lethal arms
body stuff heady stuff
ensanguined bloody powers

Two born Jews
bar mitzvah boys
recanting
daring bishops, kings and knights
maybe the Kingfisher's Gambit
 or the Queens Gambit
perhaps the Duras variation
joined with the Balogh Defense
no ditching babi yar this time
 no need for shma chanting
or tefilot on your lips
or tefilin between your eyes

Advance, retreat, advance, retreat,
Stiff little figures for armies
Capturing pieces better than persons

A strong opening for the white
 back to the 1600s
Best by test
The Ruy Opening for Lopez
Even better merged with the Black Mustang Defense
trying to read each other's minds
no looking in each other's eyes
deceptions on the board
fight for your place with your pieces.

For whose home is this game being played?
What brings them to the arena?
What the stakes?
Unarmed except by brains.
The Middle East? Europe? Iceland?
Rekjavik?
And tell me:
Were perhaps their zeydehs lansman?

The Camp

Furcated bent barbed swastikas
Twisted , knotted, braided
Tearing intervals of steel
Webs
Spun by black widow spiders
Whose prey escape solely as smoke

Through Nazi erections
Chimney stacks
Spilling seed
and like blackened teeth
snapping colorless
skies apart
barbarous belching
Black

Woven spikes
and wires from the Wermacht's
wretched war
waged against butterflies
in stripes
whose wings have no crimson left to drip

just one more stain
on thorny forked spokes
tiny darts to impale caged
flightless, colorless
unpainted birds.

Beside the Point:
Suitcase for a Guilt Trip

what happens to the birthright
not proffered?
Left aside
overlooked
in the wardrobe
in the suitcase;
never despised,
mind you
just beside the point:
exotic, quaint
baubles and beads
for the attic
for the wall cubby
there! Just there
out of reach
why climb?
Hasn't been
turned around
to be looked at
since when?
Or picked up.
Or lived.
Just there.

Family

Burying My Tooth at Auschwitz

Some time ago I returned from having visited Poland for the first time. The few weeks I spent there were a result of a happy convergence of motivations. A visit to the Czestochowa birthplace of my father and grandparents; my own age within sight of 80; my middle daughter Nurete and her two sons, my grandsons, seven and nine, Matan and Nadiv, who were able to join me in Poland from their home in Israel to spend some time with their saba driving around Poland exploring routes and roots; also an invitation to give a Sabbath talk to the Bet Warsaw congregation. They had asked me to speak to their congregation, not surprisingly, on Jewish Identity, from my book on inter and intra marriage because they had chosen to translate a section on identity into Polish and to provide a translator for my talk.

All of this came to pass. We took in Warsaw, Krakow, Czestochowa, Torun. We came across unexpected genuine interest in all things Jewish and Jewish scholarship proved to be of the highest level of intellectual study. The Poles in the cities clearly feel the great loss of Polish Jewry. And the pain is as real as the pain from phantom limbs. They don't quite know what to do about their loss. And their missing parts. But many whom we met suffer from the loss; they study seriously what brought about the deaths of the millions of Polish Jews. Moreover, Judaism is a vibrant subject: Institutes, museums, research papers, panel discussions on Jews and Jewish history every which way one turns.

Then came time for me to visit Auschwitz. I had been

to Dachau when I served as Army Chaplain stationed nearby in Nuremberg in the 1960s. But Auschwitz is different. It represents the nadir below the nadir of inhumanity and Shoah. Off to the gingerbread factory went my grandchildren to make cookies and I went off to the concentration camp. Self conscious of my apprehensions and trepidations.

Now about my burying my tooth in the soil of Auschwitz. The background is this. I grew up the war years in the late 1930s and early 40s and my friends' older brothers went off to the war as soldiers and not all came back in one piece. These were and remain the defining years of my life. I have written three books on the subject of the Holocaust. And poetry too. My Jewish theology and ideology are primarily based on sensitivity to those years and the great loss of our 6 million relatives.

For one such as myself, no longer young, it was of significant impact to walk through the camp and to see what I had already known but needed to feel and take note of with my own eyes. In a certain sense I had always understood myself to be a stepchild of the Holocaust. I did not lose immediate family; I lost cousins and uncles and aunts and their families. But a part of my soul has always bonded with all of them. Every loss pained me. I spent 9 years at Yad Vashem in Jerusalem, interviewing hundreds of survivors – Nitzalei haShoah - and working on my book, The Faith and Doubt of Holocaust Survivors. I wanted some part of me to remain through eternity with the non-survivors who couldn't speak to me as had the survivors.

I decided that I would walk through Auschwitz with a nail clipper in my pocket and when at the camp I would choose an appropriate place and clip off a tiny piece of my fingernail and bury it there and say kaddish quietly to myself. Days before I was to leave for Poland a tooth which had lived in my mouth for 70 of my 76 years emerged and came forward for the burial assignment. My dentist replaced the tooth and I took the little volunteer with me in a tiny envelope. When I walked into the display room of stacks of suitcases painted with the names of the victims and the dates of their birth on them (so they would more readily find them again after their "shower," they were told) I chanced to see the date 5/20/36. The child was born the day I was born. Had I been in Europe that could've been my own suitcase. I, my daughters, my eight grandchildren would not have come to be. Shaken, I stepped outside. I took a deep breath. This was to be the place to bury my own DNA and identify with that child and the others. And pushing the little ivory bicuspid firmly into the surprisingly soft grassy loam no longer hardened by the stomp of the Polish winter, I did. And I recited kaddish silently. I returned to hug my grandchildren later that day, dine on good Polish potato pirogue and, like the tongue unthinkingly probing the place a missing tooth had always been, sat down and put my feelings into poetry.

Routes and Roots:
With Grandsons Exploring Poland

Pesach 5772; March/April 2012
Matan, seven, and Nadiv, nine, the firm core
fixed immovable points of our turning world
there is our here when and where and ever we have
been
not so much a place in space as a makom in time
-as our heritage instructs
Nadiv and Matan, our midpoint binary
in the spinning universe
there ever where ever we are.
There is a place beyond our world where
out of and in time we share
with you the pivotal axis of our universe
as our Copernican bracha
revolving, displayed as a blessing before the holy.
Together you are the yearning and fulfillment at once
seven days and seven nights enlightened
deeply at a place where words do not reach
together we perch confidently on that calm
centered turning eye of life's storms
and earth's catastrophic upheavals
Nadiv and Matan; Matan and Nadiv.
You summon the Earth's goddesses to our side
enlightened finding our way with you in the garden
Warsaw and Kraków, Czestochowa and Torun
Routing and uprooting the lands of their sorrow
instantiating our forebears wherever we wander
refuting all sacrilege where ever we roam
with Matan and Nadiv we shall stand fast.

Dance Lessons from My Sister

A New York suburban wind
now slants, now shuffles
the single hardened rose box-stepping
beside my sister's grave. So very still;
the no longer soft loam holds fast
in the stomp of winter's sway.

When we were young
we watched cardinals, catbirds and grackles
like those feathery wings moving rhythmically
over her stone
providing secret names for them
as did Adam and Eve
in their garden and supervised
our monument-maker dad
chiseling lambs and candlesticks
pitchers for layvees
and priestly fingers
out of rock-of-ages
barre granite slabs
like this
delivered very nearly raw
from Vermont quarries.

Full skirted my sister
swirled in the glowing effulgence
of Chanukah lights singing Jerusalem verses
and golden oldies
…till the end of time
…till the mountains disappear…

Chana, she taught me to guide her

steps from the lawn
to the bungalow
our parents chose for our summers
that my feet would know
what they were doing
when I would someday ask her
to dance at her wedding.

Chana, she leads my steps still.

Cleave, Cling and Sister Chani
Taking Me Home

I cling to my earliest reveries
-ever retrievable data registering here -
Calling to mind of childhood things past
linked like icons lodged
within the keyboard of my psyche
adhering, enduring, adoring
when you were my big-sister Chani
when you were my world
when I knew you would always be taking me home.
I cleave to hand-holding treks
you to Shulamit school for the big kids
me to kindergarten at the yeshiva playground
awaiting my big sister
through very long mornings.
The sister who is to take me home.
Chani, there was no home without you
I knew no life without you
I cling to those years
when I never knew a thing without you
my big sister who will take me home
I hold on to.

Those years levitated away
floating like the errant, frisky
wind-jerked eggplant yellow
balloons with fluttering white tails
escaping my clutches
we chased down the hill
until we crumpled laughing
until we could go on no further.

I'd know that you could take me home.

We ran along as two kids run
not to where
but to when
the when a single instant
we could hold on to
cleaving, clinging
a kid brother and a little girl
who could take him home.

To a Grandson Yet to Be Born

Well shuttered until your space
gives way to the earth's own contours
created to clothe you,
a few centimeters long,
already proudly Jewish
in my daughter's womb
vestigially tailed
pre-intellectual proto-graduate student
advanced degree candidate
about ninety-days. Sounds can see you
music can see you.
Nurete your host, Mitch your sire,
I your saba introduce you to them—she a thinker, he a
doctor
she a lover, he so wise
already saving for your
schooling, ready to carry you on his shoulders
to museums and galleries walled with portraits.
Nurete, your mother, holds you close and inward.
She will teach you, *tayerl*
the joys and sorrows of speaking, reading, writing
lashon kodesh.
May you spend many happy hours with the aleph
bet
washing ink from your fingers. You will make
the walls
of Jerusalem
your own ramparts,
You will see that they stand long after I am
gone.

Who am I your saba? Something like a tree seen
through your window,
providing shade in summer, in winter
my branches heavy with snow will
skip to the wind along the hardened earth, may shelter
pussy cats and turtles
wild deer and a teddy bear
and you.

To Liam

You have been born
In my century not yours
Liam
The next century
Belongs to you.
You were born
in my country not yours
Liam
Your country is yours
Yet to be.
Your people are you, Liam
Whenever you reveal
Your name.

May you be good for your
country and for your people
May you be good
for your century.
May the me'ah be
Good to you.

נולדת במאה שלי
לא שלך
ליעם
המאה הבאה
היא לך
ליעם
נולדת בארצי
ולא במולדתך
מולדתך
כמו המאה
הבאה שלך
יהיו לך
יהיה אשר יהיה
עמך הוא לך
ליעם
בכל זמן ששמך יעלה
על שטתיך

יהי רצון
שתתרום משובך
למאה שלך
לעמך ולארצך
מי יתן
ותהיה ברכה
למאה שלך
והמאה
ברכה לך
ליעם

Hook, Sinker and Liam's Line

No academic caviling and quibbling
No coy curvatures or crumbled circumlocutionist
cutbacks
- words twisting and leaning into
and over each other.
No conspiratorially construed cliches
save for later at the kitchen stove
nodding in accord:
"best tasting fish ever."

And no palaver's pithy commentary
or poignant disquisition
put forth peering philosophically into a brooding pond
by some slick sputtering pundit
seeking the plaudits of polite appreciative applause.
Not an "I caught a fish..." copyedited report
submitted by newsboy Liam Brenner Samia, age 4.
Rather - a message, a declarative
delivered like a prophetic pronouncement:
"my first fish,
I caught my first fish, saba reeve!"
("saba reeve" affixed as a colophon inscription)
declaimed as an endearing dictum
an account punctuated not with verbal commas,
semi colons, periods, whistles, grunts and hmmms
but charged with exclamation marks
stacked authoritatively straight, erect, unbending
and tapering to a point
- resembling a cone formed by rifles
standing muzzle upward against each other -
and bringing to mind the bait casting angler's rods

likewise paling perpendicular, vertical, heaven-
pointed,
my fingers curled around and swooped up
in a single grasp exultantly, elatedly
earlier that morning .

"I caught my first fish."
A proclamation issued by chronicler Liam
with all the loving ingenuousness of certainty
and all the imaginative audacity
 of some celebrated
and excessively self-assured seer
who knows there will be – must be – more
fishing to come
with sister, saba, ima v'aba.

No self-obsessed fictioneer's testimony
faking size and weight
but an utterance echoing
ethereally eternal lines -
beaded words holding water
arranged like drops spread out on a string
and invested in the universal plainness of the
commonplace -
…grandpa…grandson…saba…neched,
precious eldest of my youngest…fishing
- catching a child's first shimmering Sunny
with baited hook, a sinker,
and a line of exquisite lyricism.

Jordan Hannah Kleiman

Flows, cascading from consecrated summits
gliding, surging, coursing
sweeping with a rushing whirl
between embankments in your element toward
wonder roiling with gracious vigor
your riverine tempest, fiercely consuming
and yet soft and tender as a woman
for whom men yearn
with worshipfully endless adoration
Jordan, cooling things like rivers
quenching conflagrations
wisdom blessed beyond years
heedful of the poetry that is your life's journey
the way an angel would lean down, Yardeni,
to hear you
attentive to your every word every need
already feeling the tug of your identity
your legacy at birthday two
paired candles invoking "shabbat" gleefully
calling with full blooded intensity
achieving unadorned radiance
and stately transcendence.
Jordan, Falling Waters,
running headlong from distant elevations
descending to your highest plane
like waves rolling down to lofty heights
tumbling waterfalls flooding Reeve's ravines
your saba too loves you, your vision
your inspired imaginings
of your promising tomorrows

with blessings realized in certainty
brachot submerged in love.

Amit

Our hearts beat
for little Amit
whether humble or elite
we are compelled to repeat
no love is as sweet
as ours for Amit.
In New Jersey 's sleet
or Tel Aviv's heat
wherever we sleep and eat
it is Amit we greet
at home or the street
you'd love to meet
Nogalon's Liamit.

Our love for Amit
will never retreat
or strike the delete
so neat our Amit
and so complete
that none can compete
with precious Amit.

Second child like Nurete
and what a treat
from bonnet to cleat
from her nose to her feet
I rain kisses on Amit.

Let me repeat
There is none like Amit.

Amit again

Defies descriptions, outstrips explanations
embodies moments of wonder and amazement
knows just what she wants
knows just what she likes
funny and friendly as your name suggests
daring to leap off imposing heights in play
trusting, brave and courageous little one
your stare penetrates the insulated mind
and strips our consciousness of all pretense.

How did you become so real, so original, so authentic
never lagging behind, never timid or shy
content to linger sidelong on notes of life's promises
as you draw your blanket up and stretch out tall
I'm moved to take your hand in mine
familiarly, unceremoniously, like a saba
and I smile that I should address you
one day to sing silly songs to you
the same verses that serenaded your mother
and her sisters your aunts
playing games of tag
running with you just for the sake of running
toward the stages of your life and toward growth
our faces uplifted to the wind
my penny words in Hebrew rattling in an old tin cup.

Amit, playmate, best friend, comrade
of mutual attachment
boon mate and companion, compatriot and confrere
accomplice in affection,
tenderly wholehearted in hesed
steadfast and true faithful friend for life. Amit.

Mayan Mayani Mine

Amen-able marvelously magnetic adept at proximity
Mayani bubbling up silvery
from some undiminished source
of healing fluid gurgling parting
the ecstatically roused waters
you erupted into our lives
bursting forth from deep spa wells,
from moistened mingling springs.

Bewitching child of my child
floating amiably, malleably
like an enchanted Hebrew lullaby
ephemeral and immortal
whose murmuring meandering moving
mystique manifests
like a mollifying melody, a symphony whose
ministering music mirrors
a manifold meaningfully harmonious cosmos.
You have made away with our every heartbeat.
And I your musing saba already memorizing
Mayan's memoirs,
Mayan's manuscript of memories, mustered
chapter by chapter
imagining Mayan as my modern emergent
miraculously materialized mitochondria.
Mayan, you are amazing.
You have won your saba's
consecrated adoration and devotion.
Mayan, mandated with every means to maintain:
"This millennium is mine:
bound and beholden to Mayan"

Matan and Saba Reeve

No rattling, ratchety grasping
roller coaster start up
ride of life for Matan.
A steady state cosmos
purposeful loco motive
speedy in motion
like a mission completed before its assignment
finding yourself with ease, Matan
you are to me like an echo report distinctly vocalized
like a hearing subtly reverberating
dispatched resounding
through the generations of our people
perceived, apprehended
fulfilled before its sounding.

Nadiv and Matan
The gift of their pledge of giving
assuring the ramparts of Zion
will be well manned.
May there be no lifelong challenge
no obsessive pursuit necessary.
Rather here because you're here
without special urgency
for a conforming required life
in some computational universe.
Not to go where a path may lead
going instead where there is no path
and to leave a trail.
Sufficient in your own justification
Matan and Nadiv, b'nai yemina strong
as the sinewy right arm

matan and nadiv
b'nai oz v'chozkei yad.
And I your Saba?
Like some hyper dimensional entity
Hovering unseen above your presence
Matan, I will be present
like in some theoretical cosmos
orbiting in a bubble universe conjured by your
gift of existence
drawn as reassuring
as vivid as steady as the gift of the trek
around our star
illuminating the track of tomorrow.

And I playful spirit intact
a plateful of resiliency
and fulfillment
satisfying my filial appetite
already tracing your memoir.

Matan, you return a part of me to myself
like the lasso of my mind
drags my own Zayde Reeven to abide in me
you lasso me one day and be
yanked along yourself one day -
so ingenious these intimations of immortality -
and you Matan a gift to me
of a cheering cheerful paean
intimating our am olam.

Matan

Always drawn toward approaching me
Like inhaling and
Always drawing away on speedy steps
Like breathing out
Your racing toward me
That one day in Cleveland
Around a tree in the front garden
remains within me.

You are what I want you to be, Matan
My horizon.

I need not ever try to see beyond you
I have no need for that
You, Matan, are as far as I wish to see.
Within your scope I scan my own.
Within your neshama
I safeguard my own.
Isn't that horizon immortality?

Talia Eden

Sparkling with epiphanic dew
source of springs and fountains and
rivers of holy lands
aqua pura as her sisters Mayan and Jordan
oceans of rainwaters cannot reach your depths.
Spray and sprinkle and soak our lives
with yours Talia Eden,
from the basin of your loving heart
from the flooded reservoir of our people's
soul coursing through the ages and through you
carrying our heritage like a timeless stream.

Wherever the flow inundates the embrace
of our banks you are there opening the harbor of our arms
to enfold you
downfalling like a brachah from the heavens
Tal v'matar sent forth tuv v'tahor
pure, frothy fine and soft like
the creamy haze of daybreak
like the foaming spray of a rainbow
tal inscribing Ya in your signature
walking wherever you will with adonai
made manifest, invoked, brought into Being
whenever you say your name
there Ya goes with you as do I your saba
kissing your fresh faultless face
entwining our fingers
as you wet the wind and scatter the rain
quickening, bracing, exhilarating
we will feel you stipple and spatter and splash
revived and restored
like the Talia mist reaching to the depths of our souls.

Noam

The story of your life
Like a pronouncement
An utterance of pleasure and pleasantness
I'd like to tell
To proclaim, to know
Noam
A joyous tale
Let it be, oh Lord
Like an eye
In the sky
I'll be watching you
Through time, the gift of gifts
Your turn, your life
Your story, no? Noam.

Within its frame
Lies the irreversible plentitude
A moment suspended
Pilfered from the continuum
And from human longing.
The many decades
Your territory
An existence with limitless duration
Your jurisdiction
Ripe for conquest
Incarnating the essence of timelessness.

Noam concentrated within herself
Staying centered
With Amit and Liam
Forever consummate friends

Sacred siblings
Am: Liam Amit Noam
Am
Your saba's consecrated *am.*

Saba's Sack

Leaping no crawling
Into Saba's sack
My grandkids
Matan and Nadiv
Amit, Liam, Talia and Noam
Little ones rolling under and tumbling over
Like overjoyed cubs and whelps springing
To bestow their love to kin and clan
Saba's sack a caper a cavort for climbing
with cousins full of frisk and frolic
Lumping on top of saba
After too much time
Without his tickles
His titillating touch, his silly chatter
Too long without his fake magic
That fails to fool
But fails not its farce, its florid flare
Its flamboyant flakiness
Can joy allude to anything else?
Once you've been there?
Once you've awakened in the morning
With little loving pats and tots
In scattered knots
Asleep beside you?
I felt their presence in a
Fleeting flitting fugitive
imperishable moment
saba and nechedim
Grandpa and grandkids
Toppling whirling plunging
Acrobats in saba's sack.

Seymour Seven Seven

SDR arrives
Come in commence command
SDR a presence
Like Herzl tall
And committed.
Take over the room
Seymour
You gain trust in an instant.
Punch it Seymour
Three sewers
Across 13th Avenue
To the corner deli
Up against
The pickle barrel
Out the school yard.
And for your next stroke
There's that flag pole's
Golden sphere on top
Hasn't been done.
Punch the pink spaldeen, Sy
And take over of the world
Why don't you?
While you are at it.
You understand
Harvard Lawman?
Why not?
You do see more
See more means integrity
And capacity and right minded,
Cogent and staunch and devoted

Armed in combat
For policies of peace
For shalom in every home
And every heart.
Shimon attentive to god's wisdom
Dovid head man and leader
Will you take a call from the president?
The prime minister?
Have you a moment for God
Seymour David
Beloved of those I love?

Once Upon Abe on Eva

Once upon Abe on Eva
begot Ricky, Helyn and Reeve a
son at last and very fast
you can believe the report
about his play and sport
(and the game he did conceive)
from Noga, Nurete and Neeva
And from Avi and Jamie
Leya, Dore - and Yariv, came he
destined for fame
so terrific his game
like his great uncle Reeve, he
faking round his opponent weaves he
the defense like a sieve,
don't disbelieve me
as for Yariv as for Reeve, see?
(What a great nephew Yariv
and what wouldn't Reeve give
To have played ball with Yariv?)
So too Greg and Ezra and Shara
(the latter in Israel now gara)
all, by your leave, athleticism up their sleeve
sporting genes from Abe and Eva
whence incomparable talents cleave
so do not grieve for Abe and Eve
the best of their pedigree did they bequeath
a legacy of smarts, athleticism and arts
that good fortune their progeny achieve.
Or so it seems to Reeve.

Amir Betrayal After Bar Mlitzvah

your vision stolen from nightmares
Amir, once himself a Jew
"I regret my bar mitzvah," you say.
Our found way re-lost
I recite yizkor for your teens.
You provide acid for the burning
of my brain.
You are a black page
within black borders
removed from
 the book of the Jewish soul:
"don't look to me to save
You in the next Holocaust,"
you say
"not here for the Jew."

You are from me disconnected
to geography wedded
gaining a land
and foregoing a legacy.
"My Arab neighbor
is my brother,"
you say
"not you and Jews
who live beyond
her borders."

Amir, choosing dirt to destiny
the new idolatry
in love with soil
in hate with those
who love you.

Soil is spelled with an i
Soul is spelled with a u
the same with dirt and duty
what is missing is the you
the Yehudi.
Amir
Get away from my daughters.

Frivolity

A Riddle Unsolved

How odd
of God
to choose
the Jews?

Oh no
it's not,
God knows
what's what.

Is the news
so odd?
the Jews
chose God.

How odd
of Jews
who refuse
to choose.

Is it the Id
in the Yid
that's odd
my God?

How odd
that Pew
defines
who's a Jew.

O my God!
how odd
the Jew
is so few.

Nu, so,
what else
is new?

Rejected Solutions to a Riddle

Rejoice
The choice
Annoys
The goys.

How odd
Of Jews
To occupy
The pews.

It's odd
When God
Is a riddle
To a Yiddle.

To a Yiddle
With a fiddle
it's God
who's the riddle.

Give the Yiddle
A fiddle
He solved
The riddle.

It's the Id
In the Yid
That's odd
My God!

(You got even
So shut up)

But not so odd
As those who choose
A Jewish God,
But spurn the Jews.

Reflections on a Heart

(lines written at Gettysburg, P.A., recalling the Nation's reaction to the coronary of President Dwight David Eisenhower)

The distant drums desist their beat
And marchers once in step deplete
Their ranks. The louder thump now turns
The pace and shuffles past concerns
Aside replacing wine and meat.
The distant drums desist their beat
As every loyal subject yearns
To hear a sounder surer heart
For fear it fail and not restart.
(While in his breast, turmoil churns.)

In towers snapping skies apart
The marchers scheme a course to chart.
At roll-top desks the ribbons glide
Above the clicking beat, as wide
Stiff collars wilt and file their art.
In towers snapping skies apart
The ticker tells on tape the slide
And climb of every pulsing vein
Which anthems loud the heart's refrain.
(While in his breast, rivals abide.)

The iron teeth chop with pain
As thousands tramp in hot campaign.
Staccatoed bursts from the fiery pump
Resound to force the frightened jump
Of soldiers clashing on the plain.
The iron teeth chop with pain
To cause a bloody lifeless lump
From men who loomed once proud and loyal,

As armies charge and then recoil.
(While in his breast, battles trump.)

The pronged forks chew the soil
As bodies bend in endless toil.
Uncertainly they plow the ground
While straining toward the other sound
 From in the mansion white and royal.
The pronged forks chew the soil
Reshaping earth to sand, and mound
Of rock to coal on which to base
The lives of every future race.
(While in his breast, a battleground.)

The louder thump new turns the pace.
And marchers pause and then retrace
Their steps to form a mute parade.
Professors drone and frown dismayed
With worried crease upon the face.
The louder thump now turns the pace.
While sprinters walk and swimmers wade
And painters rest their brush; they wait.
The marchers strut to drums of fate
That echo sounds his heart has made.

Costa Rica in June

A sleepy lagoon
neath a tropical moon
(Only a goon's out at noon)
no call to primp and prune.

Rainforest monkeys but no baboon
A Mapache raccoon
A Morpho Amathonte cocoon
An Osprey, a Macaw and a Loon
A macaque nibbling a macaroon
Nechedim in a swoon
Off key with a tune
A melody to ruin

But without you to croon?
Perhaps next time and soon.

Nixon: Abou Ben Richard and the Angel

Abou ben Richard (may his diatribes decrease)
awoke one night from a sleep lacking peace
and saw within the moonlight of his room
made rich by Gilded Lillies in bloom
an angel writing in a book of gold:
exceeding troubles had made ben Richard old
"what writest thou?"
The vision raised its head
"a list of names of your enemies," it said
then with a look made of all sweet accord
reserved for none save his Sultan Ford
and exchanging smiles one with the other
Ben Richard said,
write me as one who would bug his brother."
The angel vanished. The next night
it came again with a great wakening light
and again showed the names of his enemies, unblessed
and lo! ben Richards name led all the rest.

Lyrics Of A Litany

As a string to your lute, so am I, my people to you.
As a color in your rainbow, so am i, my people to you.
As a scout of your tribe, so am I, my people to you.
As a pigment in your canvas, so am I, my people to you.
As a flower in your garden, so am I, my people to you.
As a dox in your poly, so am I, my people to you.
As a ying to your yang, so am I, my people to you.
As a laugh in your throat, so am i, my people to you.
As a guttural in your larynx, so am I, my people to you.
As a bead in your string, so am I, my people to you.
As a coach in your train, so am I, my people to you.
As a link in your chain, so am I, my people to you.
As a step in your walk, so am I, my people to you.
As an arrow in your quill, so am I, my people tp you.
As a rivulet in your flow, so am I, my people to you.
As a clown in your circus, so am I, my people to you.
As the DNA to your helix, so am I, my people to you.
(As you may not stop here. Continue on your own.)

How Do We Know That Shlomi was Better at the Bat than Casey at the Bat?

This revelation came to me on June 3, 1988, the 100th anniversary of the publication of the poem, Casey at the Bat *by Ernest L. Thayer, suddenly, while lofting the white pellet over the left field fence, by bat, from pitch, on a rather nice trajectory, if I say so myself.*

The outlook was extremely muddy for the
      Yenimvelt nine that day;
The score stood two to four,
      With but one inning left to play.

So when Hershel popped to shortstop
      and Beryl did the same,
A sickly silence fell upon
      The chevra at the game.

A straggling few got up to go
      Leaving there the rest,
With the hope which springs eternal
      within the human breast.
For they thought: *"If only shloimi*
      Could get a whack at that."
They'd put even money with big Shloimi
      at the bat.

But Finkle preceded Shloimi; likewise
      the Schnorer Jake,
And the former was a peddler,
      and the latter was a fake.
So on that stricken multitude
      grim melancholy sat;
For there seemed but little chance,
      of Shloimi getting to bat.

But Finkle let drive a single, to
      the wonderment of all.
And the shlepper Yonkle tore
      the cover off the ball.
And when the dust had lifted, and
      they saw what had occurred,
There was Yonkle safe at second, and
      Finkle a-hugging third.

Then from the gladdened myriads
      there rose a lusty yell;
It rumbled through Yenimvelt
      it rattled in the dell;
It struck upon the hillside and
      rebanked upon the flat;
For there was Shloimi, mighty Shloimi,
      advancing to the bat.

There was ease in Shloimi's manner
      as he stepped into his place;
There was pride in Shloimi's bearing
      and a smile on Shloimi's face;
And when responding to the cheers
      he lightly doffed his hat,
No stranger in the crowd could
      doubt 'twas big Shloimi at the bat.

Twenty thousand eyes were on him as
      he rubbed his hands with dirt,
One thousand minyans applauded
      when he wiped them on his shirt;

Then when the pitcher began to wind
      the ball against his hip,
Defiance gleamed in Shloimi's eye,
      a sneer curled Shloimi's lip.

And now the leather-covered sphere
      came hurtling through the air,
But Shloimi stood a-watching it in
      haughty grandeur there.
Curving by the sturdy batsman,
      the ball unheeded sped –
"That ain't my style," muttered Shloimi
      "Strike one," the umpire said.

From the benches, packed with lansmen,
      there went up a muffled roar.
Like the beating of the storm waves
      on the stern and distant shore.
"Kill him! Kill the umpire!" shouted
      some kleegeh on the stand;
And its likely they'd have done so
      had not Shloimi raised his hand.

With a smile of Maimonidean charity
      great Shloimi's visage shone;
He stilled the rising tumult, he
      bade the game go on;
He signaled to the pitcher, and
      once more the spheroid flew;
But Shloimi still ignored it, and
      the umpire said, *"Strike two!"*

"*Gonif!*" cried the maddened minyans,
      others shouted, "*Fraud!*"
But one scornful look from Shloimi
      and the audience was awed.
They saw his face grow stern and
      cold, they saw his muscles strain,
And they knew that Shloimi wouldn't
      let the ball go by again.

The sneer is gone from Shloimi's lips,
      his teeth are clenched in hate,
He pounds with cruel vengeance
      his bat upon the plate;
And now the pitcher holds the ball,
      and now he lets it go,
And now the air is shattered by
      the force of Shloimi's blow.

Like a rocket in space
      to the distant heaven;
Way above heaven six
      and far beyond seven;
Past the cheder of the Gaon
      to the seat of the throne
Of the Almighty himself
      Mit Got's Helpf:
A black hole round tripper
      A four base ripper,
A big bang booming homer,
      Is it not stated in tractate Yoma?
And before that by the
      prophet Jonah?

Not to speak of the Masorah
on the "going, going, gona."

A gezunta blast bringing joy to Yenimvelt
that all the shreiying fans may see
It was big Shloimi at the bat –
and not Casey!

So much for the telling of this
great baseball thriller,
Now you know the rest
of the megilla.

GLOSSARY

cheder	academy
chevra	gang (a group of friends)
Gaon	Intellectual authority, academy dean, genius
gezunta	healthy
gonif	thief
kleegeh	wiseguy
lansman	townsman
Maimonidean	Maimonides was a 12th century philosopher and physician, who defined the Degrees of Charity
Masorah	tradition
megilla	scroll, story
minyan	unit or group of ten
schlepper	ne'er do-well
schnorer	parasite
shreiying	screaming
Yenimvelt	elsewhere (literally, another world)
Yoma	A volume of the Talmud
Yonkle	Jake

Reeve as Revealed with Rs and Vs

by a Rarefied Rambling rarely Revolting Reeve.
Reeve: A veritable record in revelations
of riveting reflections, reveries and reviews
Rhetorically ever revolving,
rhythmic and venerably verbal
rarely self-veneering
and nearly never reverently driven or radically riven,
Rebreeven, nor venerated,
overly revered or viewy,
As rabbi, redoubtedly rectifying, resuscitating
and revivifying the remaining Remnants.
Reeve, a Reverend
rarely reflecting an irrelevant rant or rave
His resounding vociferate and revelatory RNA
never vying for vice versa vindications
proffering a veneer of variations
vending various varieties of virile verses
resembling resplendent rhapsodic rap
reassembled as at a reverential revue
or victorious revival
reveling, revived and revving,
virtually an ever revamping Rav.
Refulgent and resonant with verve
even when redundant and reiterative.
Reverently revered by some,
reviled and venting with venom by few,
reverberant often referenced in footnotes and endnotes
and regularly ree-eve-valuating
every venture's variety of vicissitudes.
Reeve, evocatively and variably,

regularly and repeatedly revealed
as yet another reviving, vivified, vitalizing,
vivacious, volubly refined Reu-vain
the ur revealer whose venues offer revolutionary vistas
of nervy vital reevaluations.
Revivified variously and vividly
by reeve's remarkably vindicated Brenner-bravura
without bravado,
and his very virtuously and voluminously verified
and versified versions and visions of veracity.

Note on the Author

Reeve Robert Brenner was born in the Bronx, N.Y. in 1936. He was raised in Brooklyn and was Yeshiva educated. His father Abraham was a businessman who sculpted monuments and figures according to strict Jewish law and tradition. His mother Eva, a prodigious figure in the community and in family, was a housewife and so much more. They lived their final years in Israel where they are buried. Reeve's younger sister Roberta lives in Jerusalem; his older sister Helyn is deceased and the subject of poetry in this collection.

Rabbi Dr. Reeve Robert Brenner graduated from the City University of New York and was ordained at the Hebrew Union College-Jewish Institute of Religion. He served as the Senior Staff Chaplain of the National Institute of Health and as rabbi of congregations in Bethesda Maryland. He has taught in several universities including as the first rabbi of St. Vincent's College and Seminary, Latrobe, Pennsylvania. He served as United States Army Chaplain in West Germany, and in the Israeli Army Reserves. He has lectured extensively.

Reeve Brenner's articles, poetry and fiction have appeared in numerous journals and periodicals, and his *American Jewry and the Rise of Nazism* received the YIVO Jewish Scholarship Prize. *The Faith and Doubt of Holocaust Survivors*, a National Jewish Book Award finalist, is required reading in leading universities. His book, *Jewish, Christian, Chewish or Eschewish? Interfaith Marriage Pathways in the 21st Century* is available at reevebrenner.com. His latest book, *While the Skies were Falling: The Exodus and the Cosmos* updates

Velikovskian research on the origins of the people Israel.

Rabbi Brenner is the inventor of the new sport, Bankshot Basketball (and Bankshot Tennis) now being played in hundreds of USA cities and internationally. Dr. Brenner is the founding president of the National Association for Recreational Equality (nareletsplay-fair.com) advocating for sports played by physically and cognitively challenged and others differently able. *Sports Illustrated* published a feature story on Bankshot and Rabbi Brenner entitled "The Rabbi of Roundball."
He is the father of three daughters born in France, the United States and Israel. His eight grandchildren are featured in the pages of this collection. His grandchildren Matan, Nadiv, Noam, Amit, Liam, Talia, Mayan and Jordan inspired much of the poetry.

Neeva Kleiman is a linguist and a licensed social worker who currently works with children and adolescents. She earned her BA in English literature and linguistics from Bar Ilan University in Israel, and then pursued her law degree and Masters in Social Work from Yeshiva University in New York. Neeva has an extensive background in teaching and education administration. She is the proud parent of three college student daughters.